UNLOCKING THE SECRETS OF FREELANCING

A PROVEN GUIDE TO MAKING YOUR FIRST $1000 WITH ZERO FREELANCING EXPERIENCE

BY

JULIUS OMOKHUNU

Copyright © 2020 by Julius Omokhunu

All rights reserved. No part of this book may be reproduced or used in any manner without written permission of the copyright owner except for the use of quotations in a book review. For more information, address: emailme@juliusomokhunu.com

FIRST EDITION

www.juliusomokhunu.com

DEDICATION

This book is dedicated to every freelancer and entrepreneur seeking direction in their business.

ACKNOWLEDGEMENTS

Above all, God retains my eternal gratitude for the inspiration of ideas to succeed in life and to gather the experience that has helped me write this book with authority. I reserve special acknowledgement for:

Jimi Tewe, CEO of the Jimi Tewe Company, whose words stirred me from my slumber to share this treasure trove with the world;

Members of the Exponential Accountability Programme (EAP), especially my friend and brother David Echem, who created an unshakeable support system during the writing process, which was also a process of self-discovery;

My business partner turned friend, Christiana Obi, with whom I have shared all the experiences documented in this book—cheers to the future;

Ruth Zubairu, CEO of Adoza Visibility Company, for warmly welcoming my request to read and write the foreword to the book — thanks for being amazing in our first ever encounter;

Anne Bassey, who took on the task of being the first to review this book without as much as a second thought—your comments were invaluable;

Oluwaseyi Atere, my best friend and success partner, for reading everything I write and being positively critical about the flaws;

My brother and friend, Olasunkanmi Joseph, for those nights of intercession that opened the floodgates of ideas, for being the pillar on which the last phase of this work rested, and for everything in between.

To one and all, I say THANK YOU! I love you immensely.

FOREWORD

The picture of success especially online, is rarely the full picture. To attain the success you desire, you must be willing to do the work that will get you there.

Many young people are lured into underhanded practices because people they admire and follow especially online do not share how they arrived at the wealth and opulence they display. Most of them are quick to attribute their success to God and "destiny helpers".

But there is a method to the madness.

Success comes through hard work. And hard work takes time. A popular quote says "it is only in the dictionary that success comes before work". Some people might say, "there's no work". I beg to differ. My favorite book says, "Seek and you will find". If you desperately want something, you will find it.

In the pursuit of success therefore, it is best to look for models. There is no need reinventing the wheel, if someone else has done it before. This is why this book by Julius makes all the difference. He clearly walks the talk. Without being full of fluff and theory, he is willing to share his "secrets" with the world.

In today's world, strategies such as these are shrouded in mystery so that one is continually seen as an expert. Julius has chosen to build a tribe of other successful freelancers as opposed to succeeding as a lone star.

Freelancing statistics show that remote work has come to stay and more companies are embracing 100% remote teams especially with the disruption that COVID-19 has brought to our lives and businesses. The earlier you equip and position yourself, the faster you will begin to earn a steady stream of income from freelancing.

This will also be very valuable for those who believe they are multi-passionate or multi-talented. You can explore the different skills/competencies you have in order to generate more income for yourself. So you do not have to "fire your boss" in order to make money as a freelancer.

Imagine the freedom of choosing when to work and how much to charge for your expertise. There truly are no limits to your potential and when you implement the strategies in this book, the sky can only be your launch pad.

Like I always say, it is time to get seen, get known and get paid.

-

Ruth Zubairu,

Author, Content Cookbook

OPENING NOTES

The book you now hold in your hands is one of three books that detail every aspect of starting and surviving in a freelance business, with something to show for it.

After being in the freelance game for the better part of a decade, I have come to realise that many people struggle with moving away from their rigid work structures to a more flexible work system that they are in charge of. A lot of that struggle is caused by fear—of the unknown, of failure, or disappointment. That is totally understandable.

My task is therefore to figuratively hold you by the hand in this book and lead you every step of the way to where you want to be as your own employer.

By the time you finish reading this book, you will have been able to clearly document your first big income from your freelance business, regardless of whether you are full-time or part-time. I have poured by heart and soul into this book and the ones to follow, and I am proud of what has been born of that process.

I invite you to read with an open mind, and see possibilities instead of obstacles. The sky is your stepping stone, as it was my starting line.

-

Julius Omokhunu,

August, 2020.

CHAPTER 1 – INTRODUCTION

Hardwork betrays none — Hakiman Hikigaya

Defining the Relationship: freelance, telecommute, remote and work-from-home jobs

Before I go on to tell the story of how I started freelancing, let us agree on some terms used to describe freelance work. Freelancing means to hire out skills and content to a client who needs those skills and content in return for a fee. Notice the use of the word *hire* because it implies that the freelancer is not bound to the client by labour or employment laws, as with regular full-time employment. The context of the freelancer-client relationship is defined by the individual needs of both freelancer and client for a single transaction, renewable for every other new transaction. This arrangement is somewhat different from *telecommuting, remote working,* or *work-from-home*.

Telecommute jobs are jobs that you do from a distance or remotely, i.e., without being in a physical location. You can telecommute from your car, a church, a fast food restaurant, or you can choose to work from home, which is why such jobs are also called work-from-home jobs. It sounds similar to freelancing, which it is actually, but the reason I make a slight distinction between working-from-home (aka remote work or telecommute) and freelancing is because some work-from-home jobs involve a standard employment relationship between the staff (freelancer) and the employer (client). What this means, for example, is that a company may hire a customer relationship (CR) officer to work-from-home **full-time.** In that case, the CR officer will have defined working hours (maybe regular 9-5) during which he/she will work as usual but without having to be in a particular office space.

With freelancing, however, the standard practice is that the freelancer sells his skills and competencies to multiple clients at the same time and does not necessarily have a defined working schedule. After all, this is one of the perks of freelancing—the flexibility of time and other resources. A freelancer can, however, choose to take a full-time or part-time telecommute job if the opportunity presents itself and the financial reward is substantial.

In essence, the content of this book applies to freelancers and work-from-home employees at different stages of their careers. If you are already freelancing or already working-from-home for your company, or you are considering venturing into the freelance world, or about to take on remote work, then this book is for you.

I intend to figuratively hold your hand through the journey from conceiving a freelancing idea to making your first million from your freelance endeavour. The ideas and templates I share are tried and tested by me, and they have yielded verifiable results. The resources I use are also tested and trusted. With this book as your companion, you can be sure to take your freelance business to the next financial level.

My freelance journey: From zero to millions

By mid-2017, I was at a crossroads in my life. I needed to make some decisions that would alter my future and I was unsure how to go about any of it. One of the decisions I needed to make was what to do about making money. I had a contract with the largest television network in Africa that was expiring at the end of 2017 and I had made up my mind not to seek a renewal of that contract. I had decided that the mass media industry was not for me despite the glamour and potential fame. Despite my rapid acceleration in the industry, I deemed that the money in it was meagre, and I had no interest in keeping up with what senior colleagues did to get ahead financially.

So I was leaving the network for sure but did not have a job lined up, and was struggling to keep up with expenses. After a quick check on the internet, I found several micro job sites in which I could sell skills and make money. I did more research on the recommended sites and my excitement grew. In September 2017, I signed up with Upwork, Fiverr, Freelancer and People Per Hour and set about designing my profile on each platform so I could start earning money. I'm a very versatile individual, so I initially opted to sell different skills on the different platforms in the hope that one of them would 'pick up' and I would start making millions in dollars. If only wishes were horses…

My first job came from an Indian client on Freelancer. He required me to write 50 articles of 300 words each about various products in five days. It was my idea to complete the articles in five days, as I was practically unencumbered with other work at the time and was desperate to land the job ahead of other freelancers who bid for the it. The client agreed that I would complete 10 articles per day at most, and eight at least. The fee? US$35.

Project Details $10.00 – 50.00 USD

I need a copywriter who can write 50 article for me daily 5 to 7. There will be 50 topics on which you have to write 50 articles. Before bidding just remember that a sample is needed to get selected.

$1 for 500 words

Skills Required

| Copywriting | Ghostwriting | Article Writing | Article Rewriting | Content Writing |

Project ID: 15439868

*The first job I applied for

Julius O. @juliusneil2 $35.00 USD in 5 days

Writing ten articles per day, the job will be completed in only five days. An article, given the topic, will be typically completed in a hour. This means a minimum of ten hours everyday will be dedicated to the task. Done this way, results are achievable in the time frame.

My bid, with which I set myself up for defrauding

Yep! US$35 or about NGN11,000 for 15,000 words and 120 hours of work. It was an impossible task, but in excitement and a bit of desperation, I made it possible. In three days, I had completed 40 articles and submitted 35 of them when my hopes were shattered along with my heart. The client texted to say he was not satisfied with the quality of the work and was cancelling the contract as such. *Say what?* It was unbelievable. Before I could ask what happened to the quality of the work, the contract was closed and the client was gone. I was broken. All my sleepless nights in the past three days, going from house to house to charge, racking my brain in houses where there was a power generating set, all wasted.

I eventually realised that the client played me, being an obvious newbie to the freelancing business. First of all, I had applied to the job for a ridiculously low amount which suggested to the client that I had zero knowledge about what I was doing. As such, he was able to agree to that flimsy amount with me and sent me to work on a contract which was not funded. This meant that when he closed the contract, instead of getting US$35 minus the website commission, I got zilch. I did not know a contract had to be funded then. On most freelance websites, once an agreement is reached between a client and freelancer, the client has to create an electronic contract and pay the agreed sum into the contract. The money will be held in escrow by the micro job platform provider until the client approves and closes the contract. Then the money is paid to the freelancer, minus the commission. All this is trackable by both client, freelancer, and the platform owner. As my first online freelance gig, I had no idea about this. I learnt the hard way.

In anger and frustration, I abandoned my Freelancer account and moved on to Fiverr, Upwork, and People Per Hour. I sold gigs, applied for freelance jobs, and sold and applied and sold and applied over and over again. I almost gave up. My next job was not until December 2017 when I landed an editing job on Upwork. It paid US$15 for about 2,000 words. This time, I knew how to make sure a contract was created and funded before starting work. I was excited and completed the editing overnight, a full 24 hours before the deadline. When the money was transferred to my Upwork account, I felt giddy with happiness. *I did it! I did it! I did it!* Shocker. I could not withdraw the money unless there was at least US$100 in the account. *Say whaaat?*

I started calculating how many US$15 jobs I needed to do before I would make US$100 and be able to cash out. I felt discouraged again. But I had less than a month to go on my NTA contract and needed something to sustain me while I found another job. So on I went, sending more proposals, offering more gigs for sale, again and again.

In December, I found another client who offered to pay me two cents on the dollar to check their translated documents for errors. I grabbed the deal with both hands. From there, I got a steady stream of jobs which I strived to complete early so I could get paid early. It still took until February 2018 to make US$100. But when I received the credit alert from Access Bank, I was overwhelmed with joy. My effort since September finally yielded a tangible result, and that was the motivation I needed to go on.

I aggressively pursued more jobs across different platforms and although it was slow going, I was able to build up a portfolio and steady clientele. Then I was able to increase my rates per job and make more money. By December 2018, I had made a total of US$7,000 by applying the various strategies I learnt on the job. In 2019 alone, my income was around US$30,000 and it currently averages around US$2,500 a month (NGN950,000), just by using my laptop and internet in my bedroom. It sounds super fun, does it not? Well, that is because I have not written about the toil in between and the support system in place to help get to this point.

Yet, my freelance endeavour does not exist solely on freelance platforms. While I was making good money from being present online, I also had the advantage of doing business with individuals and businesses in my physical location. As far back as my undergraduate days, I was already participating in research activities for students of all levels and departments. I learnt about data collection and interpretation and I started leveraging that skill early on to make money, so it is safe to say that I started freelancing even earlier than 2017! In my final year, I contributed to no less than nine research projects for students in three departments, earning over US$1000 (NGN200,000) in two months. For someone whose pocket money was around US$25 (NGN5,000) at the time, I was freaking rich!

By the time I moved into freelancing full-time in 2017, I was able to leverage on that experience to secure jobs as a researcher/research assistant for students at various levels of study or for businesses looking to use data to make the right decisions. Business research and business development is a service I offer to this day, and it all started as a small skillset I utilised to earn small money. The idea is that freelancing is not solely an online affair. A lot of freelancers will find more joy discussing their services with people they can shake hands with over a deal than online where there is a global competition.

In the period since my first freelance job and now, I have held regular full-time jobs, completed two certificate courses, and bagged a master's degree. What does this mean? That if you make the right combinations in your freelancing endeavour, you will have full life satisfaction while making a steady income on the side. The next chapters in the book will be dedicated to sharing my experience with you on a step-by-step basis, with tried and tested tips and templates for getting ahead in a freelance business or work-from-home career.

Types of Freelancers

Freelancing is a huge business. It can be a side hustle for some and full-time career for others. So what freelancing means to you, may not be what it means to me. That's why there are different categorisations of freelancers. The Freelancers Union and one of the biggest freelancing platforms, Upwork, have come up with the following types of freelancers[1]. Can you spot which type of freelancer you are or want to be?

Independent contractor: They do supplemental and contract work on a per-project basis. Many think of independent contractors when the word "freelance" is mentioned.

---

[1] The Simple Dollar. *The Ultimate Freelancer's Guide: Everything You Need to Know About Getting Jobs, Getting Paid and Getting Ahead.* https://www.thesimpledollar.com/financial-wellness/ultimate-freelancers-guide/

Moonlighter: They've got a full-time job and a "side hustle"—like a salaried engineer who takes on consulting assignments on the weekend, or a teacher who tutors after school.

Diversified worker: Part traditional employee and part freelancer, diversified employees split their time between part-time jobs and at-will work. These types of freelancers are becoming more popular as on-demand service apps take off. A diversified worker, for instance, might work 20 hours per week as an office administrator and another dozen or so delivering goods for services like Postmates or TaskRabbit.

Temporary worker: Most of us are familiar with this subset. Temps have either a single, traditional job or a contract position for a predetermined period, like a web designer who works for three months at a soon-to-launch startup.

Freelance business owner: Think of this as a freelancer's freelancer. Imagine a successful freelance dog-walker that needs to expand her business to meet rising demand, so she hires additional freelance dog walkers. This is the type of freelancer I intend for you to become—to be so successful that you hire people in your freelance business. The idea of the freelance business owner is covered in another one of my books, *'Building Business Structures That Work.'* This type of freelancer has grown into an entrepreneur and has set up structures that works for him rather than doing all the work.

Lessons

1. Allow yourself to imagine possibilities of what might be, even amid impossibility. Sometimes, the quality of your imagination is a factor in the quality of your actualisation.

2. Your situation, good or bad, should be a catalyst for the transformation of your fortunes, whether from grass to grace or from grace to greatness.

3. It is the amount of your desire that will translate into the amount of effort you put into making your ideas a reality.

CHAPTER 2 – WHY YOU SHOULD CONSIDER FREELANCING

Life is too short. Don't be lazy. — Sophia Amoruso

Who is freelancing for?

People go into freelancing for various reasons. Most of the time, it is to earn **extra income**. It is also attractive because of the **flexibility** it affords. For those who are full-time freelancers, it is often because there are no regular jobs for them at the moment. But what most people don't know is that with dedication, determination, and a huge dose of luck (which in my case is God's grace), freelancing can be a full-time job and pay better than a regular 9-5 job, as it happened to me. I have not held a full-time job that paid me as much as I earned from freelancing per month—and I have worked on the managerial level in established companies.

So consider freelancing if the following resonates with you:

a. You desire an income stream. Freelancing is sometimes a way to opt-out of the saturated labour market. I know of some people who have consistently searched for meaningful jobs for long periods, ranging from half a decade to a full decade. There may be underlying factors in their failure to get gainful employment, but venturing into freelancing may be the only way for some people to have any stream of income and if you know your onions, freelancing may be the 'job' you live on until retirement.

b. You desire an extra income stream. Ever felt like you spent all of your salary within the month or week you received it? That happens to many people with one source of income. Freelancing can help you change that, and it does not matter what regular job you do. Many freelance platforms have a great number of PhD holders and even college professors looking for side gigs! There are websites dedicated to people with advanced degrees in a variety of fields to edit and review academic papers. Some professors act as consultants in addition to their academic work. That is a side hustle for them! Such professors are freelancing! This means that everyone requires an extra income stream, and that freelancing is for anybody.

c. You have a skill that is in demand now. Now and then, someone finds out there's a market for the skills they have—and it's not in their current employment. In 2020, for instance, video marketing experts are the rave. Do you have such a skill? Freelancing is for you.

Most Wanted Freelance Skills in 2020
AS PREDICTED BY peopleperhour
- Video creation
- Content editing
- Animation
- Logo design
- Article writing
- Illustration
- Graphic design
- Brochure, leaflet and flyer creation
- HTML expertise

d. You want more flexibility with your time. With freelancing, there's no 9 to 5 unless you want there to be. If you feel most productive between 2 a.m. and 6 a.m., you can work at that time. If your clients want you to be there 9 to 5, you can always excuse periods of absence as a "client meeting"—who's going to know? For people with families, freelancing is a huge deal! There's even a platform dedicated to moms who work from home.

e. You need more control over your life. I love making decisions uninhibited by rules and protocol. The full-time jobs I enjoyed most were those I held in managerial levels. Freelancers have the freedom to make their own decisions. There's no debating which version of a website to use or what the office dress code should be; it's all up to you. If you want to work naked in your living room or if you want to wear a suit and sit in the comfort of your garden with your laptop, you can.

f. Say goodbye to Mondays. In the 2004 movie *Garfield*, the pudgy, cute cat with a love of lasagne strolls out on a Monday, shakes the kinks from his body, and declares "I hate Mondays." As did I, and maybe you too. Well, here is a chance to take Monday off the calendar. Because whilst everyone else is suffering on their Monday morning commute (Does anyone remember Third Mainland Bridge in Lagos?), you can stay tucked up in bed or go out for an adventure without the weekends' crowds. Who's the boss?

Photo credit: facebook.com/pg/Garfield-Says-I-Hate-Mondays

Of course, for work-from-home staff on standard employment contracts, Mondays will be Mondays. But the flexibility of life and the relative lack of pressure that comes from not having a lot of colleagues around or a boss hovering over you is a deciding advantage.

g. You desire a better work-life balance. Perhaps the 40-hour week is not your thing anymore. Well, start a freelancing gig. By going freelancing, you can be sure to regain a better work-life balance. With time, you might even come to realize you only need half the time to sustain yourself and cover your basic expenses. That way, you can set up your monthly target and determine the amount of work you need to reach it. Once you reach the target, you may choose to work more or dedicate some time to your other passions, family, or friends.

Lessons

1. Knowing who you are is the first step to knowing where you want to be. Self-discovery is often the most important part of life's journey.

2. Before making a decision, ask yourself: *why do I want to do this? What do I want to gain? Is this really what I want?*

CHAPTER 3 – THE FREELANCER MIND-SET

You've got to get up every morning with determination if you're going to go to bed with satisfaction — George Lorimer

Five mind-sets a successful freelancer must (not) have

The concept of the freelancer mind-set is something I have covered in another book in this business series, *A Business Mind-set*. The concept is significant because being a freelancer or a work-from-home staff is not bread and beans. It is a demanding job that requires you to properly condition yourself in a certain manner. The mistake most people make is to see freelancing or work-from-home as an easy money venture, which it can be of course, if you do the right things at the right time. Nevertheless, having that mind-set when going into the business is a delicious recipe for disaster.

In this chapter, I will address five points that speak to the standard freelancer mind-set. Each concept, plus five others, is elaborated upon in *A Business Mind-set* as the subject matter is extensive and requires more than can be covered in this book.

Mind-set 01: Desperation

In chapter one, I shared the story of how my desperation to make money from freelancing got the better of me when I accepted my first job which ended in calamity. A lot of people who go into freelancing or receive (full-time or part-time) work-from-home job offers are so desperate to start earning that they commit themselves to deals that are not beneficial to them and are ultimately ruinous.

If you are going to start a freelance business or take on a work-from-home job, you must erase the element of desperation. Every decision with regards to working from home or freelancing needs to be taken carefully and deliberately. Most people do not realise that clients and employers of freelancers and work-from-home staff often try to lower the compensation they put on an offer when compared to if they were to hire a staff to work in a physical location.

Take for example the case of a freelancer who was offered US$5 to create a whiteboard explainer video and ended up creating two of such videos because the client rejected the first one. That freelancer was me and this was April 2018. In my desperation to get more jobs then, I offered to create explainer videos with unlimited revisions and 24-hour turnaround time for only US$5, of which US$1 was the commission for the platform provider. *Chai*, yeah? I was still getting used to the freelance business but I was bamboozled by the structure of Fiverr which started pricing freelance skills at US$5. And my initial success at getting a job or two on other platforms made me desperate to get more jobs and more money; so I priced expensive gigs at ridiculously low prices. Did I get jobs? Yes, I did, and I did them all. And after a few times, I raised my price. But those early jobs were back-breaking and I regretted doing them then even as much as I do now.

So do not be desperate. Be intentional about your goals and go about it methodically. Slow and steady, they say, wins the race. There's still some truth in this. A gung-ho approach will do you no good in freelancing or working from home. For employees of companies who work from home full-time, desperation can creep in when you set your price or remuneration during the negotiation process. Employers will claim that by working from home, you do not deserve the same compensation as someone who does the same job from an office. That is not correct.

Remember that despite working from home, you are doing the same job as someone who would be in an office, and you are probably working the same hours too—if not more. So do not sell yourself short when negotiating remuneration for full-time telecommute or remote jobs. The art of pricing and placing a value on your skillset is discussed in chapter 7.

Mind-set 02: Commitment & Concentration

It is the nature of man to succumb to distraction now and then. Many people have a problem staying focused on a line of engagement for too long, and this is a definite problem in freelancing and working from home.

The biggest commitment issues freelancers and remote staff will face is the relative lack of supervision in freelance and telecommute work. Many employees thrive in their jobs, or at least complete the bare minimum required of them in their jobs, only because of the constant supervision in their workplace environment. Anyone with this mind-set may be better off staying away from the freelance or telecommute business.

Freelancing and working from home often means that as a freelancer or remote staff, you are your supervisor. This requires you to possess extremely high levels of commitment to the work you do and a significant dose of concentration on the task(s) at hand. Simply put, a commitment mind-set and a concentration mentality are prerequisites to success in freelance/remote work.

A quick story to buttress the point. After my misfortune with the very first client I ever worked for online, I almost lost interest in freelancing. I gave up on ever succeeding in the business. My commitment to success and my concentration levels in actively building a freelance portfolio diminished significantly. The result was that for 3 months, I was wallowing in a state of flux and was neither here nor there. It took the intervention of a friend to help me recommit to pursuing my desire, but when I found the level of commitment required to polish my freelance profile, concentrate on each job I applied for, and focus on delivering the jobs as required, my workflow increased significantly.

The second book in this series contains an in-depth explanation of how commitment and concentration helped me to build a very successful freelance business. You can also listen to my podcasts on my website (http://www.juliusomokhunu.com), as I have shared several stories across the episodes.

Mind-set 03: Dedication

While they may sound and appear synonymic, I classify the dedication mind-set separately from the commitment mind-set because of the different implications. To dedicate oneself to something is to *commit to a goal or way of life*. In other words, a successful freelancer must possess ample ability to dedicate himself to a cause. This is necessary because it takes a great deal of dedication to complete a freelance task to the highest standards. And this is very important because the difference between retaining a client and losing one is the amount of dedication you put into his/her project.

Having this mind-set allows you to invest yourself to a particular task, to own the task, and complete it as though it were your job and you were the client. This mind-set allows you to commit to the goal of delivering excellence for each client.

One time, a client who teaches Forex trading in the United Kingdom, contacted me to create two whiteboard videos for his website to illustrate the feedback from his clients and to highlight the products he had to offer. He wrote me a script, sent me the graphics he had, and left a few more instructions. As a journalist with good script writing experience, I could tell that his script would not do so well for the purpose he wanted the videos for. I tweaked the script slightly without altering his original content and instead of using the low-quality graphics he sent, I edited a few of the pictures to improve the quality and sourced new graphics to replace the poorer ones. I *dedicated* myself to this project, not only because I needed to impress him, but because I could not do a job for myself with such materials. And if it was not good enough for me, then it couldn't have been good enough for him.

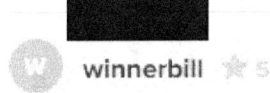 

winnerbill ★ s

The seller was excellent! He did the job to my satisfaction and even exceeded my expectation. I highly recommend and will definitely use again!!!

2 years ago

Long story short, the client was astounded by the finished work. He paid me an extra US$35 for the effort and left a five-star feedback on my profile. Within two days, I had five customers queuing up to buy my gig. A bit of dedication did that for me.

Mind-set 04: Patience

<u>Starting a freelance business is difficult</u>. That is the truth, and there is no way around it. Which is why it requires a great deal of patience. For some, luck (which I call the grace of God) may play a part and they can start flying high from the beginning. For the majority, like me, patience is required.

For those starting online freelancing on micro-jobs and freelance sites, you will require patience even while setting up your profile across numerous platforms. Each platform requires different information and it takes time to enter all that information on so many sites. It also takes time for some websites, like Upwork, to approve your account. The process can be discouraging, which is why patience is required. The same goes for people who seek remote work positions and have to apply for jobs traditionally, via email, LinkedIn, or by filling an application form online. Patience is needed.

Once your profiles are up, it requires a great deal of patience to land that first job. I must have sent at least 30 applications over three months before finding the first client that paid me money for work done. That was a challenging time, but I toughed it out and was rewarded significantly over the months that followed. Sometimes, it takes that bit longer to get the breakthrough, but the key is consistency, and patience through it all.

Mind-set 05: Consistency

A quick check on the definition of the word shows that consistency refers to *the quality of achieving a level of performance which does not vary greatly in quality over time*, and that is the hallmark of a successful freelancer.

Once you hit that level where jobs or gigs are coming to you steadily, you must be prepared to maintain a consistent standard of excellence. Many people assume that consistency is a quality that comes naturally, but it is not. It requires time and practice to develop and more time and practice for it to manifest, and yet more time and practice for it to become a habit.

It is a dangerous mind-set to assume that because you completed a five-star job yesterday that you will complete a five-star task today. Consistency is not an assumption of capacity, it is a manifestation of capacity exhibited over a period of time.

I like to think that a client worked with me for two straight years because I was consistent with my output during that time. It would have been easy to relax and assume that because the last job was a breeze, I could coast through the next one. That is the wrong mind-set to have.

How do you achieve consistency? Simply by treating each task like it is your first. See every job as if your next job depends on it—and in a manner of speaking, it does! Being consistent with your results will allow clients to trust you with more work and recommend you to other clients.

For full-time work-from-home staff, the consistency mind-set is critical. No employer is going to keep you on their payroll if you are unable to display consistently positive results. It is not permitted to be good on Monday, average on Tuesday, excellent on Wednesday, dismal on Thursday, and great on Friday. By the next Monday, you may not have a job anymore. So find consistent levels of excellence by attuning your mind to achieving five-star results on every single task. In the worst-case scenario, you may achieve a 4.5 or 4.0, but you'll be on your way to achieving a consistent record of good results.

Before starting a freelance or work-from-home job, it is imperative to prepare your mind for what to expect. Each job requires psychological, mental, and physical preparation to help you achieve success. This subject is covered broadly in the book *A Business Mind-set* and in a series of podcasts available on my website.

Lessons

1. Starting a freelance business without the correct mentality is like going to the battleground without the correct arms and ammunition.

2. Your disposition towards a task is often an easy measure of whether success or catastrophe will follow it.

CHAPTER 4 – STARTING POINTS

Start where you are. Use what you have. Do what you can. — Arthue Ashe

Identifying and defining your niche

Having evaluated the mental aspect of preparing for a business in freelancing or a career working from home, this chapter will be focused on the next steps to launching that business. I look at this from two points of view: identifying your niche and identifying what tools you need to start.

I mentioned in chapter one that I am a versatile person. This was useful to me when I started freelancing as I was able to sell a variety of skills on many platforms. But I now know, having tested multiple theories, that it is best to have a niche. Having a niche means being an expert in a specialised field rather than be smart in a variety of fields. This can be an attractive ability, but it can as easily be a disadvantage.

In a Journalism and Writing class in 2010, the late Nasiru Ikhazuagbe first introduced me to the journalism variant of the jack-of-all-trades principle. He said a journalist is *a jack of all trades and master of all*. This was an interesting insight that referred to a journalist's tendency to know a bit of everything. As a diligent student, I steadfastly held on to the ideology. I was smart and keen enough to know something about everything, which is why I was able to acquire a variety of skills that were so diverse that I could sell different skills on different freelance platforms. I did content writing, blog and article writing and editing, general proofreading, voice-over, video editing, graphics design, whiteboard animations, and even translation in MT, PTE and MPTE modes. It did not favour me for long though.

As I grew in basic whiteboard animation creation, clients began to demand more from me. I realised I did not know enough about whiteboard animations to leverage on that knowledge for sustained growth in the business. I dropped that skill from my advertised skillset. The same happened to graphics. My knowledge of Photoshop proved glaringly inadequate over time, and I found it difficult to go deeper in learning the software. I quit selling that skill eventually. Over time, I dropped all the skills I offered for sale initially and was left with a joint skillset—writing and proofreading/editing. It was in this niche that I grew rapidly, once I identified my strength in it and focused my efforts on getting writing/editing jobs and delivering excellent results. It was in this niche that I made my first US$1000. The rest, as is so often said, is history.

Identifying your niche is key to achieving sustained success in freelancing. It was easy for me to identify mine because of my training (education) and experience. I had a diploma and bachelor's degree in mass communication at the time, I had worked with the largest television network in Africa – the Nigerian Television Authority (NTA) for two years, I had been a contributing writer for two UK-based sports websites (Give Me Sports and Soccersouls), and was editor of a campus magazine for three years. Writing and editing was bread and butter for me, and they remain so. It came easy, I enjoyed it and working in that niche was neither boring nor exhausting. It was the same with writing research papers and dealing with the data from research—these were things I found fun doing and did with ease.

Now to identify your niche, you need to understand your interests as well as your cognitive abilities. What excites you? What interests you? What do you have the most fun doing? This is achievable by being self-aware. There are many tests online that help people define what their niche is, but the common theme is knowing what you are passionate about.

QUICK NICHE DETERMINATION TEST

1. Identify your area of expertise. What do you know the most about?
2. Identify what you're passionate about. What do I love the most?
3. Identify opportunities or gaps in the market. Is there actually work for me in this area?
4. Identify the crossover of these areas. Where do these 3 things meet?

Summary

Area of expertise + specific passion within that area AND/OR specific thing you love + potential opportunities or gaps in the market = your freelance niche.

Culled from Writers Edit.

Moreover, having identified your niche, you then set about defining it. Self-intelligence is a crucial aspect of defining your niche. Knowing that you are good with writing and editing is not enough to make you dive into writing and editing all written material. You must also further define what that niche means to you.

In the writing and editing example, a lover of romance fiction who writes short suspense stories for his blog will struggle to write academic articles on dark matter or the Large Hadron Collider. Can he write well? Yes. But can he write Physics? No. This is why he must define his niche. His profile can read, for example, *Creative fiction writer with experience in short stories, blog articles, and soft content creation*. Such a writer must avoid jobs that require him to write content that is too far from his capacity. Sometimes, out of desperation to make extra or quick money, aka greed, a freelancer may want to take on a job that is 'seemingly' easy. Those are the times when they get bad client feedback.

Dear reader, you have to be intentional about what you want to do and how you need to go about it. Having a skill is not the same as having all the knowledge of the industry. Therefore, if you can drive a Toyota Corolla, it is not a guarantee that you can drive a truck with cattle from Sokoto to Lagos. They are two different vehicles entirely, which is why they have different types of drivers' licences. Know where your strength is and stay on that road. Can you broaden your skillset and sell more skills and services? Damn right yes. But if your competency is not at expert level, don't take the risk.

Lastly, in selecting your niche, you must estimate how profitable that niche is or can be for you. Everyone knows that a role in IT pays far better than one in the creative fields.

The work-from-home starter pack

Once you have decided on your niche and defined it adequately, it is time to ask the question: what tools do I need to get started? Freelancing or full-time work-from-home requires a variety of tools, gadgets, and equipment if you are going to be effective and efficient.

Remember that in this line of work, your home or your base is your office. That you are a freelancer or a remote staff does not mean you are exempt from utilising certain standard office functionalities. It simply erases the need to be in the same physical space as your employer and the commute time to and from said office space. That commute time can then be spent actually working or as extra self-time.

The following paragraphs discuss what tools are required to get a freelance business started. I have also made basic recommendations for some of the tools as well as a guide on where to get them.

a. A personal computer. No freelancer or work-from-home staff can do without a personal computer (PC). It is the barest minimum, or in fact, the sole compulsory asset you must have. Now, a PC can be a desktop or a laptop depending on what is affordable or available. Of course, nowadays some desktops have better processing capacities than laptops, which means that laptops are not a sole necessity. However, the advantage of the laptop is its portability. What is the point of freelancing if you cannot whip out your working tools to get small tasks completed while stuck in traffic? In any case, what type of PC you have should be weighed against the jobs you seek/have and the skills you offer. A graphics designer or a video editor, for instance, requires a PC with higher graphics or processing capabilities than a text editor. One of the reasons I quit graphics and video editing was because my laptop at the time was incapable of handling some editing software. So, assess what you require and what you have or can afford.

Recommendation: get a laptop with above average RAM, at least 500GB HDD and 2.5GHz processor.

b. The right software. Knowing the software you need is the next best step. It is no use having a PC without what is required to make money with the PC. For some skills like writing and editing, an efficient browser like Chrome or Microsoft Edge and a word processing software like Word or WPS Writer, or even Google Docs, is usually enough. Some advanced software/plug-ins may be proofing and plagiarism checkers like Grammarly or Turnitin. For data entry and data analysis, Microsoft Excel, Power Bi, Stata, Tableau, SPSS, etc., may be the basic software requirements, in addition to a browser, of course. Graphics and audio-visual editors may need Photoshop, Filmora, Fruity Loops, Audacity, etc. The key is to identify what software is required in your niche and buy/download them. You must, of course, be able to use them.

Recommendation: research the state-of-the-art in your niche, acquaint yourself with the tools, and buy and install the tools.

c. Internet. Freelancing <u>cannot</u> and <u>can never</u> work without a reliable internet connection. Everything you do as a freelancer or a work-from-home staff requires an internet connection, which means you will be online for many hours. Those in virtual assistant roles, for instance, need a constant internet connection to respond to emails, answer calls, log events, and so on. Social media managers or online community administrators need the internet; virtual or remote teachers need the internet; virtual interpreters need the internet; editors and writers need the internet to research and share files. You need the internet to even set up a profile or submit your proposal/pitch to a potential client! So get a data plan that works for you and that you can afford. Sometimes, regular mobile data plans can be useful. I used mobile data for research, file sharing, communication, etc., for three years before switching to an unlimited WiFi plan. Figure out what works for you.

Recommendation: get a reliable internet connection. Virtual assistants and customer relationship roles require significant internet usage. Heavy file sharing may be required in the graphics and video creation/editing niche. Find an affordable data plan that you maintain while you make enough money to get a higher plan if needed.

d. Peripheral tools. By peripheral tools, I mean the extra tools or gadgets that will make working in your niche more efficient and seamless. With the first three tools, anyone can run a successful freelance business. But for some niches that involve a lot of customer/client facing via video chats, then additional gadgets may make your business more professional. For instance, a customer relationship role that involves calling customers or receiving their calls requires a good audio device, which makes an investment in a good quality headset a worthwhile one. The same applies to a virtual teaching gig, where extra lighting or an external webcam with high resolution will make the experience seamless for your clients.

e. Smartphone. Smartphones are a great tool to have for the simple reason that they are more mobile than a laptop or even a tablet. Many great jobs can be completed on smartphones, from writing to graphics design. It takes some time to master the art of using a smartphone for work but a smart freelancer needs a smartphone to make work smarter.

Recommendation: non-negotiable. Your smartphone should be put to work, making you the money to buy a new phone or PC. Maybe a car, or a house someday.

f. An ergonomic workstation. If you are going to be working long hours on your computer in your home, you will do yourself a favour by setting up a comfortable workstation. This means a desk and a chair that allows you to sit in a correct posture and access your computer. There is no use working so hard only to spend good money on painkillers or having to endure aches, pains, and bad posture. I remember my sister always warning me about being a bent-over old man if I did not get a desk and chair soon. Moreover, since I work 12-14 hours on my PC anyway, I got one and saved myself some stress.

Recommendation: very necessary. It does not have to be an exquisite setup; a place you can rest your back, neck, and shoulders comfortably while working is all you need. While you're at it, think ergonomically if you are going to set up a mini-workstation. See here for a practical guide: <u>setting up a workstation ergonomically</u>.

Lessons

1. Proper preparation prevents poor performance.

2. Failure to plan is planning to fail.

3. It is better to be over-prepared than to be underprepared. Over preparation never cost anyone anything; the thief is under preparation which is a set up to rob you of opportunities.

CHAPTER 5 – WHERE TO LOOK: FINDING YOUR FIRST FREELANCE JOB

Money doesn't grow on trees, but it grows somewhere. Where? — Julius Omokhunu

Landing your first freelance job

How freelancers land their very first job will vary from individual to individual. Some freelancers may have already completed a job or two outside their regular jobs before going into full-time freelancing. Others may already know one or two persons who need the skills and services they have to offer. Others go online and set up shop, and then build a profile from there.

Freelancers who go online to get their first client often choose this approach because there is an existing client pool that requires freelancers—even though freelancers often outnumber clients.

Getting that first job may require a lot of effort, and it may mean having to spend a great deal of time pitching your skills or services to people you think may be interested. Or you may choose to simply go online and sign up to one of the many platforms for freelancers.

Working hard is not the same as working smart, and one way to work smart in freelancing is to know exactly where to check for jobs. At the beginning of my venture into freelancing, I researched no less than 25 online platforms to sell skills on. But in the end, I started with just 4 platforms. The reason I settled for those platforms was that I noticed a high demand for the skills I was selling on those platforms.

How you get your first job and subsequent jobs depend on what you do and how much research you put into it. My recommendation is that nothing beats good old **word of mouth**. Once you have a business ready to launch, before you post adverts and run social media campaigns, it is usually friends, family, and acquaintances that will first spread the word. So tell the people in your circle what you do and what skills you have to offer. A lot of your first jobs will be from the people in your environment, and a few referrals.

Once your freelance business is about to take off, let your "people" know that you are into so and so business. That's the first platform you will have to market your services. This is something I neglected to do initially and it slowed down my progress early on. Of course, you have to be wary of the fact that friends and family often love to get free services. Don't fall for that cesspool. Everyone needs to pay for your expertise, even brothers and sisters, because business is business after all.

If you are going to start by spreading word of your new freelance service, you must be ready to pitch to potential clients and customers. Many times, these people will not come to you unless they have seen your results over time. It is your job at the beginning to reach out to them and tell them what you can do for them, how you can do it for them, and why they need you to do it for them—this is the summary of making a pitch. Remember that your pitch is likely going to be unsolicited, so you have to try to make a killer one. Many times, potential clients will not respond to your pitch but if you are persistent in pitching to as many potential clients as possible, then you stand a chance of getting feedback from one client. I have pitched to a fair few potential clients in my day with little success, but I still send a pitch every now and then if I see the potential of landing a contract with a person or a business.

Many times, finding a client without using online job boards requires you to do a lot of cold emailing. Cold emailing is to reach out to a prospective client by email and pitching your services to them. I have put together some tips on writing a great freelance pitch in chapter 9.

In today's internet world, however, there are numerous platforms on which a freelancer can sell their skills and on which to find remote jobs. I will focus on these platforms in this chapter. This chapter will save you time and energy by highlighting the nature of each of the selected platforms with direct links to each of the sites for further review. There are hundreds more than the ten highlighted in this chapter, but these have been selected because of the high rate of recruitment by clients on the platforms.

Upwork

Upwork boasts the largest job finder pool to date. This site provides a variety of jobs for every type of freelancer that could be imagined. They offer long-term and short-term projects, fixed-term or hourly contracts, and a reasonable hire success rate. Their commission rate may be quite high for newbies charging small amounts and their foreign exchange rate is quite low (US$332 to NGN1 from 2017 to 2020 without change). It is an ideal place where freelancers can market their services, offering them a highly competitive rate. They have several packages to access the pool of agencies and freelancers while making it possible for their clients to test the solution before making any commitment.

Fiverr

Fiverr is not highly recommended by a lot of freelancers because of the model with which it operates. Gigs on Fiverr start at US$5 which is really low. But it is not a fixed price, and many freelancers fail to realise that. Experienced freelancers can offer their services for competitive prices, although the presence of freelancers selling expensive services at cheap rates makes it hard to compete. It is particularly great for IT and graphics experts.

People Per Hour

People Per Hour is an online community of freelance talent that helps companies outsource specific projects to remote workers when needed. It is one of the many cloud-based platforms that are making it easier for firms to find the people they need from a global talent pool, and for freelancers to advertise their skills.

Freelancer

Freelancer.com is one of the world's largest freelancing and crowdsourcing marketplace by number of users and projects. They claim to connect over 44,076,217 employers and freelancers globally from over 247 countries, regions, and territories. Through the Freelancer marketplace, employers can hire freelancers to do work in areas such as software development, writing, data entry and design, engineering, the sciences, sales and marketing, accounting, and legal services.

Hireable

Hireable allows you to get a freelance job outside America or Europe with equal opportunity. It has a straightforward user interface and provides exactly what you expect from a freelance website: you get job alerts, recommendations, and see your saved jobs as well as the jobs you applied for.

FlexJobs

FlexJobs does not only provide a platform for freelance work, but it also encourages everyone to try this career path. Furthermore, the freelance website collects jobs from around the world. At $14.95 a month, you get full access to its wide network of employers, various skill tests, and detailed description of every company.

Writer Access

If you want to become a freelance writer, Writer Access is the best platform. It covers all kinds of writing jobs, including online articles, case studies, tech papers, etc. This freelance website has many tools such as content analytics, keyword optimization, and content planner to get more work done efficiently.

99Designs

99designs is for anyone who needs custom design and for talented designers seeking quality projects. They have a tried-and-true creative process that helps clients and designers connect and collaborate on logos, business cards, t-shirts, websites, and more.

Codeable

Codeable is primarily for WordPress jobs. If an individual is an expert WordPress developer, then Codeable is doable. Codeable offers freelancer jobs from WordPress themes to plugins. Hence, finding a new position in the WordPress niche is much more accessible now for a WordPress professional.

Guru

If you are an experienced freelancer, this is one of the best platforms for you. It is easier here to be contacted with potential employers. They give a decent amount of free applications, rationed by the year, and charge about 9% commission.

For freelancers in the African region, in Nigeria particularly, the following marketplaces provide reliable means of getting jobs and also getting a start in your freelancing business:

FindWorka

Findworka is an online marketplace for digital services and gigs, where customers find and connect with diverse, qualified freelance experts in Africa in the most affordable, timely, and secure manner. Launched in May 2016, Findworka has over one thousand freelancers onboard ranging from Web Developers, Graphics Designer, Content Developer, etc.

Jolancer

Jolancer is serving as a dedicated platform for skilled Nigerian youths to register their profiles and bid for projects in their line of expertise (skills), and for project owners (clients) to find qualified freelancers for their projects, thereby, reducing their expenses on particular projects. It works in a similar way as Fiverr.

Lesson

A person that has information will lose his way less often than the one who does not.

CHAPTER 6 – IT'S ALL ABOUT PACKAGING

IF THE PACKAGING IS GOOD - THE ACTORS, DIRECTOR AND PRODUCER - THEN IT WILL WORK, EVEN IF THE PRODUCT IS NOT GOOD. — NUSHRAT BHARUCHA

Making yourself attractive to clients

Decided on a platform yet? Awesome. Are you going to send pitches to potential clients? Fantastic. Next question: how do you start attracting the clients? The trick is simply in the packaging. How you organise your profile online and offline is always going to be a huge determinant of how clients will perceive you and how often they will even hold conversations with you over a job.

In regular job hunting, a well-prepared CV that showcases the applicant's strong points, attached to a properly worded cover letter, will make a strong impression on the recruiter. The same applies to freelance profiles. The difference between a successful freelancer and a struggling one is often the amount of time and care they both take to set up their profiles—to 'package' their profiles. I learnt this over time. As I researched about freelance profiles and how to make them great, I tweaked and re-tweaked my online profiles and my offline portfolio. I experimented a lot until I settled on a profile outlook that I liked, yet even now I tweak my profile from time to time to reflect new experience, or new skills and qualifications.

How attractive your profile is depends on how well you package it. Packaging a profile means presenting your top selling skills in the most eye-catching manner possible.

Setting up an online profile optimally

When setting up an online profile, it is best to optimise your profile with the keywords and skills related to the projects you want. Clients will often find freelancers by searching for the keywords in the projects they have—web designer, experienced graphics designer, etc. With that in mind, zero in on keywords and skills related to the projects you want and the services you offer. Staying consistent with the skills you choose to highlight will be important as you fill out or update those parts of your profile.

Title: Be descriptive about the services you offer. Highlight your primary talents instead of trying to include every skill you have. Remember that while you want clients to know you're "hardworking," "reliable," or "passionate" about what you do, you need to save those for your introduction, overview, or description.

Introduction/Overview/Description: Most online platforms provide a section for you to describe yourself in more detail. This is where you will have the opportunity to sell yourself to the client that clicks on your profile. Remember that your title has attracted them to see more about your profile; now your overview needs to give them something to think about. Upwork, for instance, recommends that you *write a short, concise, and to-the-point summary—no need to reiterate the skills you've already listed in the tags above. Instead, expand on them and explain what is unique about you or your agency, including the types of clients you've worked with and the technologies or industries you specialize in*. This is crucial and because only the first few characters show up in search results, try to keep it brief.

Skills and Experience: Different platforms have different structures for entering data about your skills and experience. The first thing you want to do is study how each platform works. However, what is common is that you only need to select the skills you wish to sell and all subskills and complementary skills. For instance, if you are selling data entry skills, you are also likely to be able to do virtual assistant jobs because both jobs go hand-in-hand. Virtual assistants often do a lot of data entry tasks but both data entry and virtual assistant may be different skill categories on different platforms, so don't hesitate to select both skills. In the experience section, treat this section in the same way as you would your CV/resume. Take time to highlight your most relevant experience, highlighting the achievements you've made in each role. Freelancers make the mistake of assuming clients do not read profiles, but they do! Some platforms even give you insights into profile views. Monitoring such stats can show you how effective your profile setup is.

Education/Certifications: For some skills, educational qualification is not relevant. For others, it is a necessity. Jobs that have to do with reviewing scientific articles or even writing doctorate level papers or researches require a certain level of academic qualification. The bottom line is to flaunt it if you have it. Even for skills that do not require academic qualification or certification, enter whatever qualification you have. I once landed a freelance job because I had a university degree, not because I necessarily had a special qualification or the needed experience. So populate this section with all the education and certifications that you have. What you should NOT do is lie about what credentials you have just to get a project.

Now, remember, while preparing and packaging your profile, your key task is to make it appealing to a client and for it to reflect your core competencies. Don't make the mistake of under-marketing your ability by simply stating the obvious. Take your time to indicate what skills you have, what projects you completed successfully using those skills, and what credentials you have to back them up.

A writer, for example, is guilty of under-marketing if he simply says "I possess good writing skills" and "I have written several articles for several websites." Adequate marketing of his skills will be more like "I have excellent writing and editing talent, with particular passion for legal content and have completed several big writing projects for XYZ.com, ABC.org, and JFK.com." If there are links to certain projects, put them on your profile. Some platforms have a portfolio section where you can upload your past work. If you have any, upload them. If you do not, then don't bother much. I didn't have a portfolio on my profiles when I started freelancing, and in fact, I still don't. I only share a portfolio with clients if they specifically request it.

Lastly, you MUST try to COMPLETE your profile to 100%. The difference between how high your profile will rank in search results and how often a client will consider you for a project may lie on how comprehensive or complete your profile is. Take time and energy to ensure your profile is completely filled in. It will be worth your while.

Building an optimal offline profile

As not every freelancer will start freelancing online, it is important to learn how to create an offline profile for yourself before you start making pitches, sending proposals to potential clients, or seeking telecommute jobs.

An offline profile is a kind of profile you build for yourself that is not dependent on the structures or limitations of an online freelance marketplace. This often requires hard work and persistence as it means you will have to connect with a lot of people just to build that visibility around yourself and what you offer. The key to being successful offline is in being **visible,** and that interestingly also sometimes means you will need to have profiles on online platforms like LinkedIn. The difference between a profile on Freelancer, for example, and one on LinkedIn is that the former will connect you directly to (remote) jobs while the latter will connect you to (remote) people with whom you can do business.

Whether you choose to target jobs in a competitive marketplace or target people who will connect you to jobs, you need to be appealing to the owners of the jobs and the people that will connect you to the jobs. Building that appeal lies in being visible, being noticeable, and being noticed by the people that matter to your freelance endeavour. How can you build up that profile with the people that matter? Let us take a look at five possibilities.

Networking. Networking might be a frightening thought to some people because of the need to interact with strangers, but it remains a cutting-edge way of generating leads in your freelance endeavour. That is because it can often be a lot easier to forge a personal connection with a potential client if you meet face-to-face. People are often interested in dealing with real people, rather than documents sent in the form of emails and PDF attachments. Where you go to for the purpose of networking is very important. You have to identify which events your potential clients attend and find a way to get in—seminars, clubs, and other similar events are a good place to check. For instance, if you write copies for businesses or design e-commerce websites, you may want to look out for entrepreneurship conferences or annual conventions near you, and attend in whatever capacity. Your clients are most likely to attend such meetings and you can always introduce yourself to them. Networking is also a good way to connect with freelancers who do what you do, to help you build a network of people you can rely on as you make your way up the ladder in freelancing.

LinkedIn. LinkedIn gives freelancers the advantage of instant connections and getting your pitch and work directly in the face of people who make decisions that matter to you. Leveraging on LinkedIn requires that you spend the time to build an engaging profile and connect with the people that matter. LinkedIn breaks down barriers between you and the clients you need. It is also a known fact that professionals and business people are happier to engage with a service provider like yourself on LinkedIn rather than responding to cold emails or calls. You must also be active on LinkedIn, as you are on regular social media like Instagram and Twitter. LinkedIn is on this list of optimal offline profile building because it is not a job board site—especially not for freelancers—but it can connect you to the people that can hire you for freelance projects, or even full-time remote jobs.

Use people you already know. This means of growing your profile offline requires you to leverage on the influence of the people already in your circle who would like to work with you or refer you to others. Start by telling your existing connections of your new freelance business, and you will be surprised how many leads you will get from there.

CHAPTER 7 – PRICING

F*CK YOU. PAY ME. — MIKE MONTEIRO

What you need to know about prices and pricing

A very key aspect of completing a freelance profile is pricing. Pricing is the financial valuation of the asset and value which you offer as a service to the people who so desire that service. The most important aspect of pricing is perhaps the most overlooked—value. In freelancing, you will be competing on value and not on price. This is something I did not get right initially. In my early experiences in freelancing, I sought to compete based on price by reducing what I charged for my skills. It fetched me a few jobs, but the income from all those jobs combined was not worth the actual price of one.

Clients often prefer quality over cheapness. Much like a coach or a tutor, a freelancer will never have a loyal following or client base if they do not create and offer value. The key to nailing pricing is in providing value first and foremost. I have had clients tell me to take a longer time than I proposed to complete a project, even if it meant they would pay more money. While the goal of a freelance business is profit, the emphasis should be on ensuring that the product or service is so valuable that clients will be willing to pay whatever it takes to get that product or service.

Having created a product or service of value, what rates do you charge for the services you offer? How do you balance being affordable and being competitive? What do you need to know not to sell yourself short? These are critical questions. My experience in the early days offered me some insight into how not to go about it.

An early mistake I made was to offer my skills and services for dangerously low prices just so I could stand a chance of getting jobs ahead of other freelancers in my field. It worked initially (Remember the US$5 whiteboard animation videos and the 50 articles in 5 days?) but I quickly learnt that I was cheating myself horribly. I was getting paid a tenth equivalent of the work I was doing. It was hard. But it had a purpose, even if it was poorly executed in the end.

I would often consider that clients would be scared away by huge prices, even if I was certain that the amount I was thinking was worth the service I was going to provide. I often ended up accepting around US$78 (NGN30,000) for research activities that would last around 3-4 months and would ideally have cost around US$100 for each month I worked on those jobs. The problem is that I doubted the value I was giving to clients. This often happened when I had to deal with clients I met physically through referrals and when I bid for jobs online.

Remember that at the beginning I was new to freelancing and to many of the online freelance marketplaces. There were already thousands of freelancers on the platforms before I joined and I needed something to help me get ahead and get jobs fast. My strategy was to sell my skills very cheaply. I may have ended up selling those skills too cheaply but it got some clients on board, gave me experience on the platform, and the clients ended up leaving rave reviews on my profile. Ultimately, I could afford to let the quality of my work and the feedback of satisfied clients to speak for me when I negotiated other projects. These days, I can afford to turn down certain projects if the price is less than what I am asking. Those early days seem so far away now. ☺

What works for you may not work for me, and vice versa. I strongly recommend against under-pricing yourself just to get clients come to you. After a while, I realised that clients will pay premium money if you convince them of your worth. In this light, experienced freelancers may have an edge as they have their past works to show. However, your pricing should be the average going rate, and not below.

How to get pricing right

The first step to pricing your services is research. A quick Google search will tell you what others in your field are charging per project or per hour on a variety of platforms. Some freelance platforms even have guides on how to set your price. Endeavour to read such material to give you an idea of how clients on the platform behave. Also, check out other freelancers' profiles to see what they charge generally and per project. This will give you a basic knowledge of how to begin.

Next, consider what work you will be doing frequently. How much would be adequate for you to do such work without regretting it? Write it down. If it is a fixed price, consider your effort, the commission you will have to pay to the freelance platform, and probable withdrawal costs. Do you want to factor that into the price you quote to a client? If it is an hourly job, consider how much work you can do in an hour. How many hours would it take to complete the basic tasks you will have to do? Then write down a number. Enter this number in your profile as a guide to clients when they come looking. For instance, your profile may show that you charge US$35 per hour. It will tell a client with a US$5 per hour budget to look away.

Now, remember that what you have on your profile may be different from what you bid for a job with. For instance, your profile may read that you charge US$35 per hour, but when you apply to do a project, you can bid US$25 or US$40 depending on the specific nature of the job. So always price each job on its merit.

To use pricing to get ahead, you may remove 5% from the going market rate when you quote your price, maybe even 10% but only as it is convenient for you. Never make the mistake of pricing a US$200 job for US$50. The result will frustrate you.

Also, remember that most of these freelance platforms process payment in US dollars. You need to be aware of the latest exchange rates when you quote a price. Use that to finetune your pricing. A US$1000 project may not be tempting enough for a freelancer in Chicago, but a freelancer in Mombassa, Kenya can afford to take on that same project for US$800 and still be happy with the proceeds he gets. Keep these differences in currency translation in mind. And don't also forget the percentage of the commission of each platform. Some charge as high as 25%, so ask yourself if you really want to take a hit on the cost of the project and take a further hit when the platform takes its commission.

Above all, never lose sight of the fact that you are providing a service that is of value and nothing should encourage or force you to place a low estimate on your value.

Lessons

1. Healthy self-esteem is important to properly place a value on your skills.

2. Never underestimate yourself or sell yourself short. Your skills are a product of sweat and tears, do not be ashamed to demand a premium amount for it.

3. Beyond the money you expect to charge for a service rendered, ask yourself if you would pay yourself what you are asking a client to pay.

4. Value attracts reward quicker than begging does. People will naturally gravitate faster towards your service if they can see your value than if you merely ask them to pay for an average service.

CHAPTER 8 - USING ONLINE JOB BOARDS TO YOUR ADVANTAGE

THE LONGER YOU'RE NOT TAKING ACTION THE MORE MONEY YOU'RE LOSING. — CARRIE WILKERSON

Approaching clients on online job boards

Most freelance platforms work in such a way that contact between a freelancer and a client is initiated by the freelancer. The model is such that a client would post about a job, stating the requirements and the nature of the job. The freelancer sees the job via a search and applies with a proposal of why he is the best person to complete the job. This is much like a regular employment search.

The first contact is at the proposal stage. When sending a proposal to a client about a job they have posted, you must take care to send in your best proposal. Proposals often include several parts: proposal, fee, duration, project type, and others. **The proposal** is the text area where you write what you have to offer, to convince the client you should be hired. Writing a winning proposal will be discussed below. **The fee** is how much you desire to charge for the project. In addition to the tips on pricing given, remember that yours is one of many bids for the same project so you need your fees to be competitive. **The duration** is how long you estimate that it will take to complete the project. A day? A week? A month? Up to six months? Be realistic about your capability. Don't put yourself under undue pressure by claiming the ability to complete a project in a duration you cannot realistically achieve. But also remember that <u>clients appreciate freelancers with short turnaround time.</u> **The project type** refers to whether you are bidding to make this a fixed project or an hourly one. Often, the type of project is determined by the client but the freelancer can negotiate this at the point of submitting a proposal. Remember that the goal is to find a mutual ground of satisfaction. When I say **Others** I mean that some clients may require you to answer some questions or provide certain details in your bid. The following job descriptions, for instance, have subtle tests and mandatory questions. Can you spot them?

> More details:
> - fully remote
> - contract-based
> - preferably commission-only (15% recurring in total for the affiliate manager and his/her influencers), but we might be able to agree on a monthly retainer fee with recoverable draw to get started
>
> IMPORTANT: Start your application with "I Read The Job Description" so that we know you did...

Sample 1: The test in the job description above is a test of attention to detail.

> **You will be asked to answer the following questions when submitting a proposal:**
> 1. Why you and nobody else? (What do you know that others don't?)
> 2. Your detailed process (no illegal, spam, black hat lead gen for instance)
> 3. What do you need from us to perform best?
> 4. What tool can you use (and how would you rate yourself for each of them from 1 to 10)?
> 5. Track record (specific KPIs) and achievements, if any?

Sample 2: How carefully you respond to these questions is more important than the cover letter you will submit.

Be sure to carefully read the job post and attend to all the requirements before submitting.

Submitting a winning proposal for a freelance project online

Proposals or cover letters are vital if you are going to land a job as a freelancer. There are millions of freelance jobs posted every day and it takes something extra to get you to the top of the pile; one of the most common ways is to pitch a proposal to the potential client.

Let it be known that there is no sure-fire way to write a winning proposal, but a combination of tips and tricks will help you get there.

- Do not copy and paste a template: this is a no-no. If you are doing this, then stop. Maybe copying and pasting a generic proposal is more time-efficient, but it is also significantly more ineffective. You are more likely to find success if you write a short but very relevant and specific proposal than a lengthy, generic one.

- Keep your proposals short: no one likes long block of texts, especially if they have so much to read. Go straight to the point and KISS it! (Keep it short and simple.)

- Try to capture the client's attention immediately: Andreea-Lucia Mihalache[2] notes very importantly that *"you have just a few seconds to win your client's attention, so you need to be witty in the first two or three lines. One trick I use is to look at the feedback on the client's [...] profile when applying; other freelancers will call them by their first name in the feedback. This lets me start my application with their name. By doing this, I leave the client wondering how I know their name, which draws them to my profile to see if they know me. It also shows that I am very interested in the job and in collaborating with them; I paid attention to their job description and looked even further. Finally, it makes the application more personal."*

- Restate the client's problem: after reading the proposal carefully, restating the core of the problem tells the client that you understand what it is he wants, and that attracts him to your proposal.

- Tell them why you are the best fit for their project: many freelancers make the mistake of talking about themselves in their proposals. This is what I have done. This is how many years of experience I have. Basically, me, me, me. That's not what

---

[2] Andreea-Lucia Mihalache. How to Create a Proposal That Wins Jobs. https://www.upwork.com/hiring/for-freelancers/how-to-create-a-proposal-that-wins-jobs/

clients want to hear. The proposal below is an example of a badly written proposal, despite how organised it is and how interesting it looks. Take a look at it.

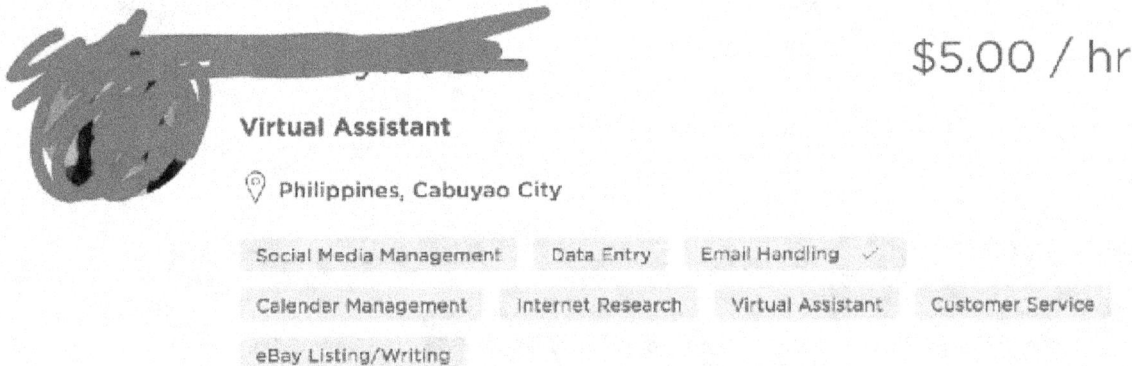

$5.00 / hr

Virtual Assistant

Philippines, Cabuyao City

Social Media Management   Data Entry   Email Handling ✓
Calender Management   Internet Research   Virtual Assistant   Customer Service
eBay Listing/Writing

Cover letter

I am a well-rounded virtual assistant.

A responsible and dependable Customer Service Representative for 5 years, I had worked for telecommunications and retail accounts and obtained expertise in placing orders, service recovery for orders, billing, device troubleshooting and obtaining details of complaints. My experiences in a high-pressured environment have taught me attention to details, resilience, and flexibility in using different tools provided by the client. I am hard working, good listener, fast learner and adaptable to meet my employer's timezone. I value my client's trust and I commit myself to any job, taking full responsibility in completing projects on time.

My skills include:
* Call Handling
* Email Management
* Calendar Management
* Office Applications
* Internet research
* WordPress
* Social Media Management
(See portfolio items below)

I'm looking forward to helping you grow your business by sharing my experiences and expertise and learn more in the process.

Now compare the above with this one below. The difference is that the proposal below speaks to the needs of the client, with a reinforcement of the proposed services by relevant experience. Importantly, it provides a stage-by-stage outline to the approach and then tries to engage the client by asking the question: do you have any questions for me?

Cover Letter

Hello! I see that you need some help offloading and upgrading some of the financial processes in your growing business. I can help with that and can start right away!

I'm a great fit for this role because as a fractional CFO, my goals are to help you create streamlined processes that free you up to do what you're awesome at, while I handle the day-to-day financial tasks. I've consulted with dozens of small businesses and have started, run, and sold businesses of my own, so I know first-hand the challenges of wearing every hat in the building. I can help make your life easier by taking some of the load off of you.

If we were to get started, here's how I would approach this project:
1. Chat with you to determine pain points and processes that need improved and offloaded.
2. Prioritize the above to get as much off your plate as possible as efficiently as possible.
3. Document all new processes and systems, so that it's very clear what's getting done, who's doing it and on what schedule.
4. Once we establish the new processes, I would look for ways to optimize this and save you even more money by taking some of the more administrative tasks and delegating them to my team (with your approval, first). Once stable processes are in place, I usually try to save my clients money by assigning some of the ongoing management to my team, who operate at a lower rate, to save you money.
5. Over time, we'll continue to try to find ways to make your life easier and improve.

Do you have any questions for me? less

📎 AlbertCo.AccountingChecklistforMonthEnd.pdf (162.68 KB)

Source: https://medium.com/@mikealbertdotco/how-to-write-a-proposal-on-upwork-that-actually-gets-you-hired-93f0434bebf9

Tip: If you land a contract to do a project, it is very important to ensure that the client pays the agreed amount up front into the designated escrow account. Avoid clients that ask you to start work before they fund the project, or clients that ask you to work for them outside the platform even if they promise to pay you via the platform or via an alternative payment means like PayPal.

Lessons

1. Make a strong introduction in a proposal.

2. Sell your strength.

3. Anticipate and answer the client's questions before they are asked.

4. Include relevant samples in your proposal.

CHAPTER 9 – FREELANCING OFFLINE

I DO WEDDING VIDEO ON THE SIDE, AND I ATTEND BRIDAL SHOWS, MEET BRIDES, GROOMS, AND OTHER VENDORS, AND BOOK A LOT OF CLIENTS THAT WAY. — SEO CLERK

Approaching clients offline

In chapter 5, I talked about cold emailing as one of the ways to reach out to clients who are not exactly after your services. But cold emailing or direct emailing requires you to put in a lot of hard work in tracking down companies and individuals you would like to work for, obtaining a means of reaching them (in this case via email, but it can also be by direct mail), and then writing a custom letter to each one (your pitch). Laura Pennington Briggs, author of *Start Your Own Freelance Writing Business*, suggests that "making a list of brands you'd love to do business with or people you know you'd like to forge a personal connection with can be a good first step."

Briggs also states, "with a carefully written, personalized pitch, you'll have a much better chance of a person reading and responding to your email. You should always test things out though and set a number-based goal for cold email pitching. Your pitching skills will get better [over time] and you'll also learn what type of subject lines and pitches work overall from how many people are responding to you or opening your email."

Writing a Great Pitch

The first thing you need to remember is that your pitch is completely unsolicited, which means you need to have a super attractive pitch for your prospective client to even give you a second thought or reach out to you. While there are many different ways of writing a pitch, the following tips are a sure-fire way of putting together a pitch that will contain all the elements that a prospective client will desire to see. Ultimately, whether you get a call back or reply from a prospective client is dependent on several other factors such as whether the client does need your services at the time or if he is having a bad day. Your part is to write a great pitch, and here's how:

A). State the prospective client's needs: this requires you to do serious homework, but if you are not up for the rigour then you are probably not up for freelancing. When you pick a prospective client, you need to figure out what they need that you can provide. A web designer, for instance, can identify that a business's website is outdated and needs new elements to make it contemporary. The business (let's call it Julius' Apparel) may indeed need a new website but the management has not realised it yet. State in your pitch that you think that designing a new website or updating their current website and including certain new features, such as new payment channels, is a necessity that needs to be acted upon. This shows you are interested in the business and you have done your homework. Clients and employers often like to know their contractors or employees are interested in them.

B). State why you think it needs solving NOW: remember that you have done your homework, so you can tell the prospective client (Julius' Apparel in our case study) that x percentage of shoppers in the Julius' Apparel's target demography now prefer to make purchases with, for instance, cryptocurrencies. So Julius' Apparel risks losing a part of its customer base to competitors such as ABC Clothing and XYZ Fashion, which have both incorporated cryptocurrency as a payment option for customers.

C). State how you can help solve the need: this is where you state your capability—what you can do for Julius' Apparel to solve its need. Maybe you can redesign the website such that the new payment option is the first option customers see when they check out? Or you could recommend that info about the new payment option be put on a banner at the top of the website? Ultimately, write down what unique solution you are offering, after all, there are hundreds of web designers.

D). Elaborate on why your solution is the must use: given that there are many solutions available to the problem/need that you may or may not have rightly identified, why must Julius' Apparel use YOUR solution? Is there an added value that you are offering? A discount, perhaps? Or a free month of web management after the close of the project? Convince the prospective client of why you are the real deal.

E). Use numbers where applicable: people can relate with numbers a lot. If it is applicable, talk figures. Let the prospective client know what your service can do for their business or profile. For instance, you can mention (with some research, of course, not some bogus claims) that Julius' Apparel can retain its customer base and attract about another 2% of customers from x and y demography if you are contracted to build a new website that incorporates the features that appeal of its current customer base and the x and y demography. Be creative, but truthful.

F). Talk about your experience, if you have it: sometimes, you may be pitching your skills for the first time and hoping to land a first client—that is okay. Steps a-e is already 99% guaranteed to keep the prospective client interested, especially as you have shown an interest in the client previously. But if you have experience in executing similar projects, you have to flaunt it.

G). Talk about yourself: I have mentioned somewhere in this book that people like to deal with people, and not experiences. So talk about you, what you are about, what your personality brings to the service you sell. Talk about your people skills, the feedback you have gotten, and why you are a 'nice guy.' This can be a good replacement for the experience section if you have no experience.

H). Conclude with a call to action: leave the prospective client with a decision to make. Ask for a call back or a reply for elaboration on aspects of your pitch. You could ask the CEO of Julius' Apparel how excited you'd be to work with him directly on the project, especially as he is such an enthusiast about making shopping easy for buyers—and you know this because you checked him out on LinkedIn or Instagram (@juliusomokhunu).

I). Above all, KISS it: clients are busy and won't be interested in reading lengthy, unsolicited text. So when pitching to a client, keep it short and simple. While you weave all these points into the pitch, let concision be your watchword.

With pitching, Briggs, who authored the very good book *Start Your Own Freelance Writing Business* notes two points which I'd like to repeat here. She says not to expect an instant response, and this is true. "People will fall off the process at every stage of your pitching. From opening the email and responding to it, to scheduling a call and all the way through to a signed contract, the pool of people who will work with you shrinks at each stage," so keep an open mind when sending in your pitch. You will likely have a low response rate, but no one ever said pitching guarantees clients!

Briggs also notes that one mistake freelancers make is not following up enough. "If you pitched one person once, and that's it, no wonder you're not hearing back. It can take dozens of pitches to get a response, and you may have to follow up for a long period of time."

Getting a Project Done

Congratulations on landing a freelance project! What's next? Well, get on the job, that's what.

Having negotiated a favourable contract, it is time to get the job done. Some freelancers can quickly become overwhelmed with the weight of a project the moment they have to commence work. This is why it is very important to agree on reasonable deadlines with the client—it will give you the latitude to work at your pace.

Here are a few recommendations for tackling a project:

1. Work carefully, not in a haste. Start the work on time, take pauses in between to keep you fresh and alert to limit fatigue and the errors that come with it. Pacing yourself is important to delivering a finished product/service of high quality. This is why it is important to agree enough time to enable you to finish a project without going right down to the wire.

2. Invest time and effort in the work. View the project as your own; put yourself in the shoes of the client. Do the extra where possible, but never go out of the agreed specifications. By investing your time and effort and owning a project, it is easy to veer away from what has been agreed between you and the client. Take care for this not to happen. While you try to over-deliver, always work within the client's framework. And when in doubt, ask questions.

3. Always communicate with the client. Many artisans, like web designers, have a reputation for 'ghosting' (being suddenly unavailable) once they have landed a

contract. Most times, it is not the case that they abscond, rather that they work in some form of isolation. But in remote work, this is not a good practice. Until you have built up a certain level of trust, you must maintain communication with the client while you complete their project. This also includes asking questions, making recommendations, and seeking their approval to do things differently than agreed. Some platforms even ask clients to rate freelancers based on their communication skills. But don't go giving unnecessary updates about the progress of the work; a minute-by-minute commentary is not necessary.

4. Deliver on time. Again, punctuality is a measure of a freelancer's quality. It is very important to work with agreed deadlines and to promptly notify the client if delays are likely to occur. Remember that a client is putting a lot of faith in you without knowing you from the Garden of Eden. Delivering their work on time is a good way to build trust. Now and then, circumstances may arise that cause you to miss the agreed deadline. Inform the client respectfully and ask for more time, preferably a specified amount of time. *Tip: Never accept "urgent" jobs if you are not 100% sure you can deliver when needed.*

5. Ensure you deliver value for money. One of my favourite sayings is that "people will buy anything—as long it has value." And it is true. Perhaps, I should write a whole book about creating value for sale. But while providing a service to a client, your emphasis should be on delivering value for whatever money they are paying. Value means giving them exactly what they want and what they need—and then some.

6. Working from home is not for every freelancer; some people find it convenient while others find it distracting. You need to know what works for you. I find it easy to work from my house but that also depends on the company I have at a particular point in

time. This is why I am a registered member of a private library that gives me a quiet working space with internet facilities. I often use that space when I have certain projects to complete and the ambience at home is distracting. Do you also need external working space?

CHAPTER 10 – GROWING YOUR FREELANCE BUSINESS

To be successful, you have to have your heart in your business, and your business in your heart. — Thomas Watson, Sr.

Retaining clients and getting more work

Expanding your client base is not the only way to grow and improve your freelance business. Sure, the more clients you get, the more money you will make. But it is possible to have only a few clients and still have a nice revenue stream. The longest I have worked with a client is 2 years and counting. During this time, we have built a relationship founded on mutual trust and understanding. I get a steady flow of work from the client and try to steadily deliver quality output. I'd like to think I've done a good enough job so far, as I still get jobs on a 1 per day ratio, approximately.

Retaining a client is a good way of getting steady work, and this is particularly useful if the client is a business owner or an agency. Some agencies/businesses rely on freelancers for 90% of their work processes. While some agencies/businesses hire a different freelancer for every new task/project they have, others prefer to find a freelancer they are happy with and stick with them for long-term cooperation. So there are lots of jobs waiting for you out there.

Clients appreciate that you have gone above and beyond for them, and they will remember. Some of them have been disappointed by freelancers in the past, so when they find a diligent and honest freelancer they are very happy to show commitment to such a freelancer.

 **Julius** @JuliusOmokhunu · 10s
"Make your clients so happy and successful that they become your sales force." @pjrvs ryrob.com/why-freelance-... via @theryanrobinson

In the same way that clients have been disappointed by freelancers in the past, freelancers have had their fingers burned by clients too. So before trying to establish a long-term relationship with a client, you need to be sure that the terms of the agreement (even if it will be informal or unofficial) are suitable for you.

Julius @JuliusOmokhunu · 4m
"Choose freelance clients that'll help you get to where you want to go."
ryrob.com/why-freelance-... via @theryanrobinson

What's the key to retaining a client and getting more work? It is basically about doing an excellent job the first time. Let's look at a few points.

Deliver excellent work. This is the first step to catching a client's attention. Having done a fantastic job for a client, you may sometimes need to do nothing more than that. The really appreciative ones will express their satisfaction and state a desire to work with you again. When your work engagement is via an online platform, it is easier for clients to express their satisfaction or otherwise because most platforms provide that feature. I have received many leads that were successfully converted into sales by delivering work that made clients work with me repeatedly, and many more sent work my way. One time, I packaged a seminar presentation for a postgraduate student. The work was so good that his colleague at work contracted me to essentially write every content he needed for the presentations he made at work. I made cool cash every week for six months because the first work I delivered was near perfection.

★★★★★ 5.00 Oct 2018   Fixed-price

Excellent work. Julius is very accurate and thorough in his translations. Doesn't hesitate to go the extra mile for clients. Highly recommended and we definitely continue to work with him!   < Share feedback

State your availability for more work. If you sufficiently impress a client, it is easier for you to tell them that you will be willing to take on more work from them as you enjoyed working for them. Never be shy to ask for more work, but don't beg. Simply mention politely that you will be very happy to do another job for them and leave it at that. If you are lucky and the client is happy, they will come back with more projects.

Request a positive review. Most freelance platforms allow clients to give public feedback about freelancers. The easiest way to get positive feedback is by doing a good job and making it easy for the client to write feedback like this:

> Proofreading of one document st $545.00
> ★★★★★ 5.00 Sep 2018   Fixed-price
> I have used Julius a couple of times now. All I can say is his work is of   ⌲ Share feedback
> the highest quality, his turnaround is quick, his price is reasonable and
> competitive.
>
> Very highly recommended, he does what he says he can do. The best
> person I have used on Upwork

Some clients may not be so bothered though. In that case, don't be hesitant to ask for a good review. As you end the communication thread (hopefully temporarily), chip in that you'd appreciate the client leaving a review on your profile as it will help you grow your business. Many clients are happy to oblige once asked, so don't be silent and let a good review pass you by. A lot of good reviews on your profile will open the doors to new jobs.

Follow up. Sometimes, clients will forget they said they would send more work your way—but you must not forget. You will have to follow up on such clients at a later date with a friendly message or email "just to check-in and see how you are doing" and "thanks again for the opportunity to work on your last project." Many clients appreciate the follow-up. Sometimes, they may still not have anything for you to work on but it does not hurt to use the technique. Be careful not to send too many messages to a client after your contract is over though. One message after a reasonable interval is enough, and leave it at that, if the feedback is unfriendly.

Try to get referrals. Good, old-fashioned word of mouth is still the best bet to get more clients and more work. Online, this translates to previous clients mentioning you to their friends and colleagues and encouraging them to contact you for their projects. Depending on your relationship with a client, you can politely ask for them to kindly refer you if the opportunity arises. Many will be happy to help your freelance business grow. Offline, you need to tell your friends and family of your new business and ask them to tell their friends and the families of their friends. You will be surprised how many leads you will generate from there.

Have a good customer relationship skill. Clients will remember an excellent customer experience as much as they will remember good delivery on set objectives. Your communication skills have to be top-notch, as a result. The quality of your words will create a lasting impression on their consciousness, so you need to pick them carefully. Communication is an art because of the beauty of expression that follows from the process. But it is also a science because there are precise ways of executing a communication exchange to achieve maximum results. My course on the art and science of communication will arm you with the skills and knowledge to engage your clients meaningfully and maintain a good relationship with them for your benefit.

Network. Networking is crucial. As a freelancer, you need to connect with other freelancers in your line of work. Join groups and be active in them. This will not only get you more work, but it will also help you with industry information when you need to fix your prices, take on new clients, or acquire new knowledge.

CHAPTER 11 – MANAGING YOUR GROWING BUSINESS

IF YOU SIT ON YOUR PROGRESS, IT WILL RUN AWAY FROM YOU. YOU MUST RE-INVENT THE WHEELS CONSTANTLY. — JULIUS OMOKHUNU

Managing workflow

Hopefully, you can build your freelance profile to the point where you can get multiple jobs coming in at the same time. In the past, I looked at some freelancers and was impressed that they had four to six projects running simultaneously. I often wondered how they did it. Now I know. In my freelance business, I sometimes get three or four projects on the same day with different delivery dates. I accept them all, mostly because I have mastered the art of managing workflow.

The desire for every freelancer is that they have a business so big that they can live off of it. Well, that can happen. The moment you start feeling inundated with work, it is a clear sign that something is changing in the dynamics of your economic situation. At that time, you must be careful to manage the increased workflow carefully or you might just as easily be back to the start. A few tips on managing workflow include the following:

Create a project map. A project map allows you to keep track of what project is at hand, what you need to do and when each project is due. This will help you stay organised and also guide you in negotiating deadlines with clients.

Don't bite more than you can chew. In the first paragraph of this chapter, I mentioned that I accept all jobs that I receive, no matter how many they are. That is because I have worked out a system that allows me to do so and still maintain the quality of my output. My advice is never to take on more projects than you can handle. Weigh each project on its merit, and decide if you can deliver on the targets in the time specified. If the answer is no, turn it down. You do not want to do a wishy-washy job and harm your reputation just for a few extra bucks.

Outsource. This is a very viable way of getting a lot of projects completed and making some extra bucks on the side. I do this sometimes with my writing projects. Outsourcing means to accept a job and pass on the responsibility of doing the job to another competent person while you share the fee for the job with the person. Outsourcing is a very delicate affair. First of all, you must have complete confidence in the competence of the person to whom you are outsourcing a project. Their failures are yours to take on, so you must know them and know their work. Secondly, you must review the work done before delivering to your client. Be sure to make any corrections where necessary. For design projects, you may request for the source files so you can make edits. And lastly, you have to accept that for jobs you outsource, you only get a small percentage since you are not doing the job.

Start an agency. If you become so successful to the point where jobs are flowing in nonstop, you may choose to start an agency. An agency allows you to have a team, perhaps even a remote team, with whom you can share projects as they come. Some of your team members may be independent freelancers on their own, but having them in your team means you can have a go-to person when projects that you cannot handle come in. Setting up an agency is a simple, yet complicated process but it may be worth it if you need the extra hands to handle the workflow. An agency may also be set up if freelancers with different skills need to work harmoniously to complete a project. So an agency may have team members with a diverse range of skills which means they can attract specific project types or more complex projects that require multiple competencies. The revenue sharing in an agency is different from when outsourcing. Some agencies share revenues evenly, some have some kind of percentage sharing formula or a pro-rata sharing plan. Others have an incentivised model where a team member gets a bonus for bringing a project to the team. Do what works for you.

Work in a partnership. I have saved the best for last—but it is what's best for me, so be sure to stick to what works for you. I started online freelancing by teaming up with a partner early on. We have maintained that partnership to this day, and the results have been nothing short of phenomenal. The way partnerships work can differ, but my partnership with Tiana is one that plays into our individual strengths and enhances the quality of work we do. We work on aspects of projects that we are best in so that the finished product is excellent, because our emphasis is on excellence. Unlike outsourcing, partnerships are effective because there is a binding agreement or mutual understanding on how work and money is shared. Partnerships also allow you to save time from seeking other freelancers to outsource your work to, because you already know who to call. And if all the partners are actively seeking work for the team, it means more inflow of work and more money for everyone. Partnerships, however, do not work all the time. They are best when both partners work in the same niche and can easily divide tasks, like writers and editors, rather than writers and web designers.

How to protect yourself when working offline

Freelance work is usually very rewarding, and quite secure when working on reputable platforms like Upwork and Freelancer. However, it is possible and sometimes necessary to do some work outside of these platforms—to work offline. Many of these platforms advise against working for a client offline, and rightly so. For clients and freelancers alike, there is the possibility of being scammed of money or work.

Conversely, one could argue that these platforms ensure that work remains on the platform simply because of the profit they earn from their commission on each project.

I have worked with a couple of agencies offline, and I have been burned precisely twice, but not since 2018. My first recommendation is to, as much as possible, keep all jobs on the platform where you met the client. What this means is that payment and contract terms should be documented on the platform before any work begins anywhere else. However, where it is necessary to bypass the platform entirely, the following tips will be useful:

Research the client thoroughly. If you must work with a client remotely, without the protection of freelance platforms, you need to do your homework very carefully. Research the client on the internet, check their website, social media pages, etc. If it is an agency, check independent review sites like TrustPilot to see their rating and how others assess them. This will give you an insight into what kind of client you are dealing with.

Understand their payment system. Different clients, especially agencies, have different payments systems. It is your job to know what each client works with. Some clients pay immediately after a project, others have a payment term of 10-45 days. Some require you to submit invoices, others do not. Some only use PayPal to pay you, others have the option of bank transfer. These are details you need to know before agreeing to work 'offline.'

Make sure to sign a freelance contract. This is a no-brainer. Even for clients with whom you have worked a long time, it is absolutely necessary to sign a contract when taking your work outside a secure platform. Mind you, some clients will require you to sign contracts, mostly confidentiality agreements, even before they hire you on a freelance platform; that is normal. But for offline work, it is a necessity. The contract must reflect the nature of work to be done, the payment to be agreed, and the term of payment. Every detail of your work needs to be reflected in the contract. Take time to read the contract and be sure to raise objections to sections that do not sit well with you, or missing terms.

Consider your first job an unpaid test. As a way to avoid disappointment, I often consider the first project I complete for a client a test. I do not place a lot of expectations on the fee. How a client behaves with the first job is often a picture of how they will treat you in the long run. Sometimes a client will exceed the agreed payment term by several days or weeks, or they will cease communication when the project is completed and delivered. Even if they pay what they owe eventually, it is a signal of how the relationship is going to be going forward. Do you really want to continue such a relationship?

Always have proof of work. Some clients can be cunning when it is time to pay what they owe. Some may like the quality of your work but will threaten to withhold payment over flimsy excuses such as failure to meet a deadline by as little as an hour! Some will even cancel the project after you have completed 95% of it. That's heartbreaking, and I know because I've been there. That is why proof of work is important. There are project monitoring systems that can record your every step in a project with time stamps. You can also take screenshots of your work at intervals as proof if need be.

Ask for advance payment. Depending on the duration and scope of a project, it is very normal to ask a client to make an advance payment on the agreed fee. Sometimes, you can even charge the full fee upfront especially if it is a small project. The advantage is that you ensure clients do not change their mind midway and cancel the project or even claim to be dissatisfied with the finished work just to avoid paying you. And even if the project is cancelled after a point, you will still have gotten paid a fraction of the agreed amount. I work in milestones on long projects. I request for part payment after a certain portion of the work has been completed, and when I receive the funds, I transmit the part work.

Establish a billing system early. If you are working offline without the protection of online platforms, you will find that many clients and agencies that will hire you have a specific invoicing system. This means that you will be dealing with multiple systems of invoicing. How about you create your own system and ask clients to agree to it at the negotiation stage? The difference between the invoicing processes for different clients is the payment term. Some pay immediately the project is completed, many pay after a period ranging from 5-45 days. You may not have a lot of control over this, but you can control how you keep track of and bill clients. A lot of systems are available out there, and if you connect with me on my social media pages, I will be more than happy to guide you in making the right choice.

Bonus Tips to Keep Your Freelance Business Thriving

1. Have a visible presence online, take for instance your portfolio website.

2. Diversify your business if you have a variety of skills and competencies.

3. Consider setting up a registered business if your endeavour grows beyond what you can manage independently.

4. Follow the trends in your area of expertise.

5. Consistently reinvent yourself by learning new skills and applying them to your projects.

Closing Notes

Wow! Thank you for taking the time to read through this straightforward guide to building a thriving freelance business. I am excited for you because you are about to become wildly successful in your chosen niche.

The question most people ask me is *what do I do now?*

I do hope that before reading this book to this point, you have already created a plan for getting your business off the ground. If you have, then **congratulations!**

If you haven't because you are still having doubts or you need answers to specific questions, that's okay too.

Whatever stage you are in, I am here to guide you on to the next stage. If you need help with:

- creating a business growth strategy
- preparing a business plan for funding/investment
- designing and implementing a marketing communication project
- increasing visibility for your personal brand or business
- targeting specific audiences for your business
- establishing an online presence via a website and other social media
- coaching on business idea generation
- proposal/pitch preparation

All you have to do is reach out to me and we will take your game up another notch.

Connect with me on:

- LinkedIn at Julius Omokhunu
- Instagram: @juliusomokhunu
- Twitter: @juliusomokhunu

Or send me a message at emailme@juliusomokhunu.com

I look forward to hearing from you.

Your partner in growth,

Julius Omokhunu

Julius Omokhunu

www.ingramcontent.com/pod-product-compliance
Lightning Source LLC
Chambersburg PA
CBHW080940220526
45465CB00008BA/3100